The Day Time Stood Still:
The Hurricane of 1915

By: Wayne Norwood

Louisiana Treasures Museum
Copyright 2015

Book Dedication:

For the victims of the 1915 hurricane and Mrs. Helen Schlosser Burg ...may their story never be forgotten.

The Day Time Stood Still:
The Hurricane of 1915

Finding Your Way Around

September 29, 1915 started off as just another ordinary day for the residents of Ruddock, Wagram (Napton), and Frenier, located in south Louisiana. Life along the shores of Lake Ponchartrain was peaceful, quiet, and quaint. As farmers harvested their crops, ladies tended the laundry, and children played in the yard, a soft breeze blew off of the lake. Clouds rolled in during the day, but no one paid them any mind whatsoever. However, their way of life would forever be changed before the night was over.

Living along the shores of Lake Ponchartrain was nothing new for these families. Their ancestors had settled the area hundreds of years prior. The area was first explored in 1699 by Iberville. Around two hundred years afterward, the French and Spanish explored the Lake Ponchartrain area in 1802. These explorers told about large cypress trees with moss, different species of fish, and about Indians of the area in their writings. These documents were written in French and Spanish and were later translated by the Louisiana Board of State Engineers on March 15, 1939.

The entire area was later occupied by Germans. But where did these German immigrants come from? On March 7, 1721, a ship named Partefaix brought three hundred German colonists to settle in Biloxi, Mississippi. The commander of the expedition was Charles Frederick d'Arensbourg. After facing many hardships, the German colonists left Biloxi and settled in a small village in St. John the Baptist Parish called Lucy. The original name for the town of Lucy was Karistein.

The German colonists gradually moved around, and in the 1800's, many settled along the shores of Lake Ponchartrain. In 1854, the railroad found its way through the area and aided the German colonists' way of life.

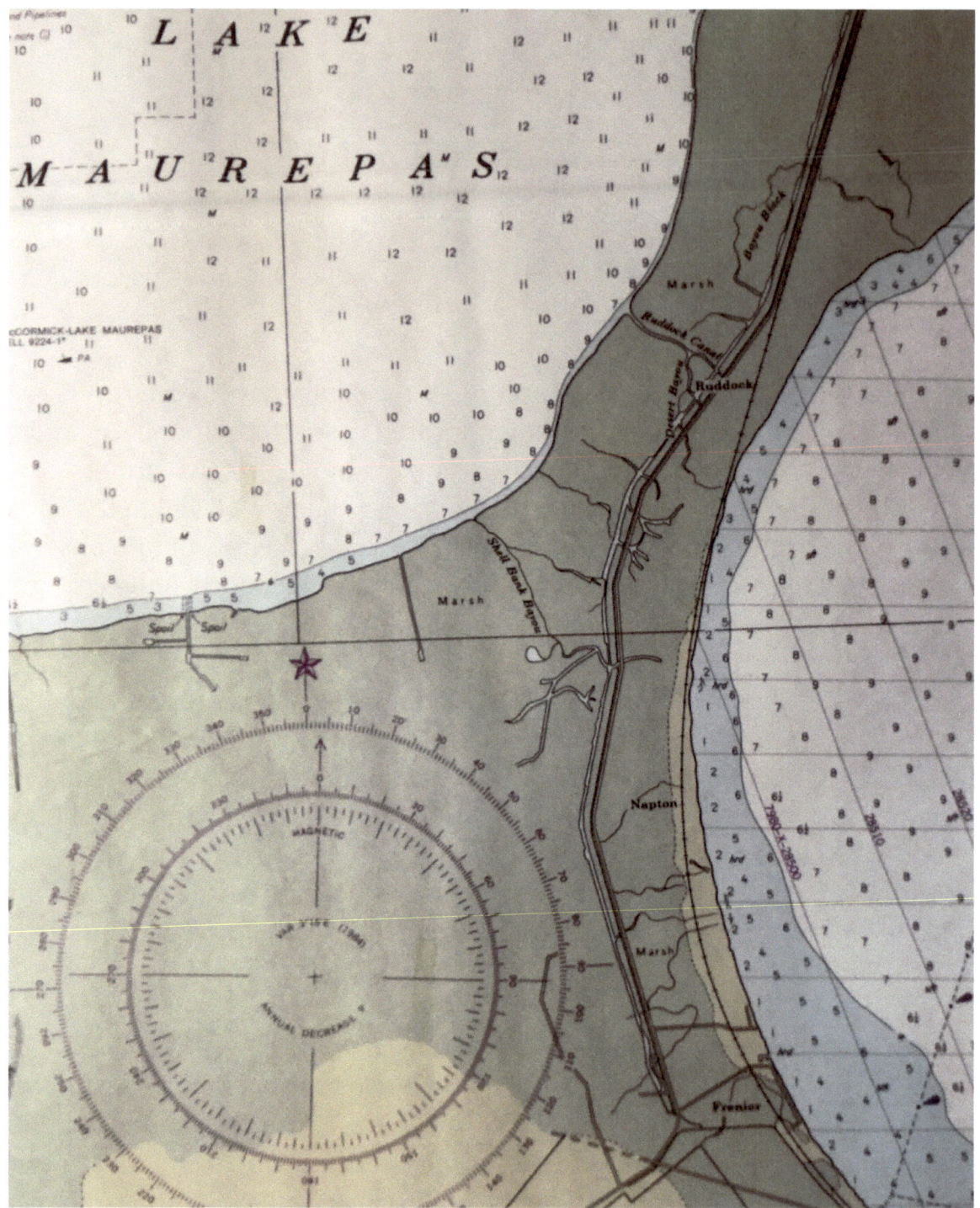

Map of Lake Maurepas and Lake Ponchartrain area. Map shows location of Ruddock, Napton, & Frenier.

Photo: Louisiana Treasures Museum

The railway went from New Orleans to Chicago. Before the railroad, these families had to send items on a ship across the lake. And without roads through the swamp or stores nearby, the railroad made buying and selling of goods, as well as travel, much easier and faster.

So where were these settlements along Lake Ponchartrain? If you are heading south on I-55 from the Manchac exit, known for the famous Middendorf's restaurant, Ruddock was the first and only town along the railroad and was located at mile marker 880.6.

Ruddock was a sawmill town with a population of about one-thousand residents. The town of Ruddock was established because of all the cypress trees waiting to be cut down. The Ruddock Cypress Company was incorporated on February 26, 1891 in New Orleans. According to mortgage book #444, page 146, the Ruddock Cypress Company owned over three-thousand acres of cypress trees and swamp land from South Pass in Manchac to the area of Frenier. Unfortunately, in 1903, the Ruddock Cypress Company caught fire and burned to the ground. Thus, the Ruddock Orleans Company was formed by means of a merger with the Orleans Cypress Company.

So, what did Ruddock look like? Ruddock had a telegraph office, post office, train engine shop, and an express office. The post office for Ruddock was built on November 12, 1891 and dedicated on July 15, 1912. There was also one boarding house that was owned by Mrs. Ulrich who was German and spoke German as well. A spur off the main railroad track went to the west where the train engine shop was located. The spur then continued almost a mile west through the swamp and onto the sawmill.

The houses at Ruddock were on the east side of the tracks and were all two-story homes. There was a main walkway down the middle of the street, which was a slab of cypress cut and laid in the swampy area for the residents to utilize. Houses were on each side of the walkway, and a community center was located at the end.

TOWN OF RUDDOCK 1900

The thriving sawmill town of Ruddock in 1900. Now, it's only an exit off I-55 and a boat launch.

Photo: Louisiana Treasures Museum

When you left Ruddock and headed south along the railroad track, the next train stop was called Wagram. Later, the name was changed to Napton. Napton was located at mile marker 885.5 and was not a town, only a train stop.

Mrs. Helen Schlosser Burg, a storm survivor, said that everyone who lived south of Ruddock were farmers and would work their fields all day long.

"Every day at 1:00 pm, the people would go into their homes and take a nap from 1:00 until 3:00 and rest. The name of Wagram was changed to Napton because of this," Mrs. Burg said with a little laugh in her voice.

There were no other towns south of Ruddock. Houses were scattered along the railroad track. Some were almost ¼ mile apart. All of the houses, with the exception of a few, were on the east side of the track and all faced the track. From each house to the railroad tracks, a dirt walkway was used. The walkway was raised about two feet above the swamp and was about four feet wide.

The farming community started a few miles south of Ruddock. The location of each house and who lived there has never been made known to anyone, until now.

I was given this information on February 22, 1990, and I have not revealed it to this day. Since this is a very special anniversary of an extremely deadly hurricane, now may be the time to tell of these heroic people.

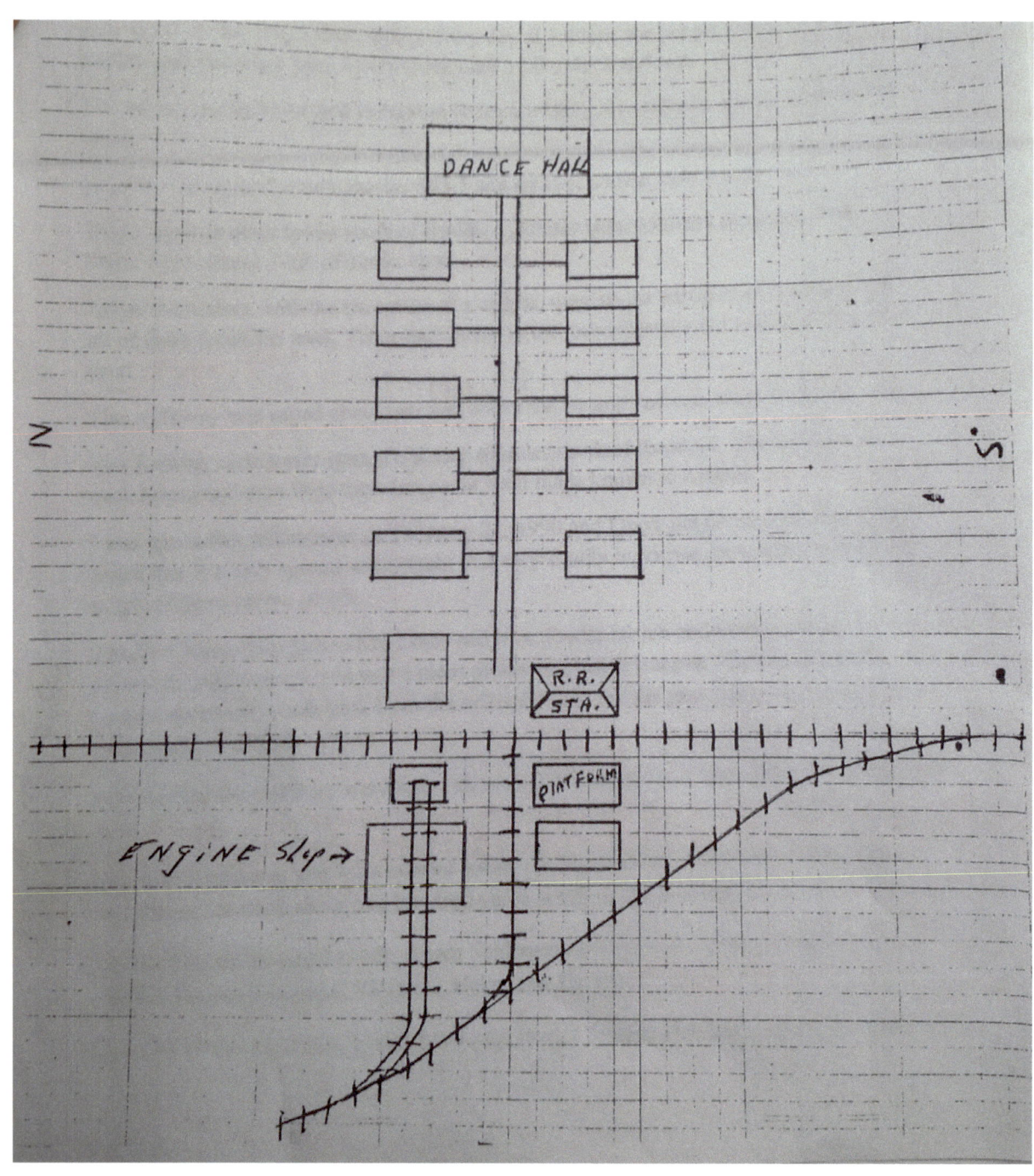

Map of Ruddock in 1900 as described by Mrs. Helen Schlosser Burg.

The Manchac train depot in 1903.

Photo: Louisiana Treasures Museum
(Courtesy of Tom Davidson)

MRS. HELEN SCHLOSSER BURG
1901-1990

Mrs. Helen Schlosser Burg (1901-1990) survived the storm of 1915.
She was able to share her story right before her death.

Photo: Louisiana Treasures Museum

People of the Past

Mrs. Helen Schlosser Burg was like a walking history book. Her memories of her childhood were as clear in 1990 as they were in 1915. She was able to identify the people who lived in the area at the time of the storm. Mrs. Burg was also able to describe where each house was located in Napton and who lived there. These are the heroic, courageous people who witnessed one of the worst hurricanes in the Lake Ponchartrain area. Some survived, however; most did not.

The first house belonged to Mr. Louis and Mrs. Fredia Ulrich and their children, Elizabeth and Henry. Louis was a moss picker and also a trapper. Their house was located about 100 yards back from the railroad track. The graveyard was west of the track by about twenty-five yards.

The second house as you headed south belonged to Mr. Joe Ferrant. The house was east of the track and about two hundred yards south of the cemetery.

The third home belonged to Mr. Adam Schlosser and his wife, Mena, along with their children, Emma, Lawrence, Florence, Helen, and Cecille. This was the home of Mrs. Helen Schlosser Burg's family. Her home, along with all the other homes, faced the railroad tracks with Lake Ponchartrain located in their backyards.

Just across the track and a little south was Holy Cross School and Holy Cross Church. The cemetery located in Napton was surrounded by four large oak trees. Many Civil War soldiers, along with residents of the area, were buried here. Today, the abandoned cemetery is overgrown with trees and weeds. No headstones mark the burial site either. Only locals know its existence and location. It's as if time has forgotten this lonely resting place.

The next house, number four, was for Mr. Matthais Schlosser. His wife died earlier, and he lived there with his children, Jacob, Martha, Mary, and Cecille.

House five belonged to Mr. Theodore and Mrs. Lizze Grode and their children, Willie, Freddie, Charlie, Sophie, Harry, Robert, and Margaret.

The sixth house was inhabited by Mr. Harry Grode and his wife, Mena, and their children, Martin, Louise, and Hazel. Their home sat behind a railroad platform along the tracks.

House seven belonged to Mr. Matt Grode and his wife, Lizzie, and their only child, Salvadore.

The eighth house was for Mr. Martin and Mrs. Mary Schlosser. They had no children.

House nine belonged to Mr. Frederick Kirch and his children, Johnny, Freddie, Barbara, and Maggie. In the front yard of their home, large pecan trees were nestled next to the railroad tracks.

The tenth one was the home of Mr. Windecker. He built his home after a storm in 1909. Mr. Windecker lived there with his wife and children, Joseph, Adam, Henry, John, Martin, Charlie, George, Maggie, Annie, and Lena.

House number eleven was the home of Mr. Adam Schlosser, Sr. and his wife along with their twelve children. Mr. Schlosser was born in 1823 and was from Germany. He went by the nickname of "Black".

And finally, house twelve belonged to Mr. George Schlosser and his wife, Margaret, along with their children, Lydia, Frank, and Lizzie. Mr. George Schlosser's home was located at Frenier at mile post 888.2. The distance from Ruddock to Frenier was a little over eight miles.

Ruddock had all of the houses located in one spot, like a small town. But when you left Ruddock and headed south, the houses were spread apart for an eight mile area.

Over the years, people called the area where Mr. George Schlosser lived, Frenier. But, in 1915, there were only three houses in that particular spot. One house was for George and his family. The second house belonged to an African-American woman named Aunt Julie Brown. The third house belonged to an unknown African-American family.

From Collection of
Tom Davidson
Hammond, La

The Napton (Wagram) depot along the tracks was nothing fancy. Since Napton was not a town, a bigger depot was not needed.

Photo: Louisiana Treasures Museum
(Courtesy of Tom Davidson)

Left Photo: The area of Napton is pictured. Yellow grass above and the barren area indicate where homes once stood in 1915.

Right Photo: Shoreline near the Napton cemetery where residents were buried after the storm.

Photos by: Wendy Woods

Frenier became a small village after the storm. In the 1920's, just five years after the deadly storm of 1915, people moved into Frenier. It slowly became a lakeside resort. A large bar was built, along with fishing camps. Peavine Road in the Frenier area was built in 1926 and connected to Highway 51. People came from far and near to fish, swim, boat ride, and enjoy the lake.

Now, there's an interesting folktale that goes along with Aunt Julie Brown. According to local legend, Aunt Julie Brown was presumed to be a Voodoo priestess. She was known to have cursed the entire swamp area from Ruddock to Frenier. Stories tell us that Aunt Julie Brown loved to sit on her front porch and sing songs. One particular song told about the day she died and how everyone was coming along with her.

Well, the day before the storm, on September 28, 1915, Aunt Julie died. During her wake, the hurricane arrived and the storm surge killed those in attendance at her bedside, along with most of the residents of Ruddock, Napton, and Frenier. Coincidence? Maybe so.

Now, personally, the tale is just a story at best. Mrs. Burg never claimed Aunt Julie to be into Voodoo or anything else suspicious. I believe it's a great story told to tourists who take a swamp tour and those looking for adventure. As a matter of fact, a swamp tour does take you to a makeshift graveyard, marked with the year 1915. Tour guides tell all about the storm and the legend of Aunt Julie Brown. However, the graveyard is a prop, for its location is nowhere near Frenier.

The entire area seems a bit cut off from the rest of the world, so, why would anyone want to live in such an isolated area? Well, the residents took great pride in their land and knew of no other place that they wanted to call home. Way of life along the lake was hard at times, but it was a good, simple life. Families and friends had been connected for hundreds of years with a bond of determination and love. That very determination and love would soon be tested in the most extreme way.

A photo taken at the mock graveyard set up as the burial site of Aunt Julie Brown and the victims of the 1915 hurricane for swamp tour purposes.

A hurricane was approaching without warning. The residents along the lake had no time to prepare, no time to evacuate to higher ground. Their survival would depend upon nothing other than luck and the grace of God.

September 29, 2015 will mark the 100 year anniversary since this dreadful hurricane came onto the shores of Lake Ponchartrain. It's a story that has never been forgotten, however; new information never released to the public will be brought to light.

Through the eyes of a survivor, Mrs. Helen Schlosser Burg, the hurricane of 1915 comes to life once again. As she clung to little pieces of paper with notes written on them, Mrs. Burg recalled that fateful day, like it was yesterday...

Photos taken at the actual Napton cemetery. Today, the area is abandoned and overgrown. No tombstones mark the dead buried here.

Photos by: Wendy Woods

A Survivor's Story

The story you are about to read is a true story. It was told to me by Mrs. Helen Schlosser Burg, who was there and lived to tell about the storm that struck St. John Parish on September 29, 1915.

Mrs. Burg was born in the little area of Wagram (Napton) in 1901. She had a vivid memory of the deadly storm that struck that night. She sat down with me one afternoon, allowed me to film her story, and answered a lot of questions that I had about her life in 1915.

On the shores of Lake Ponchartrain below Manchac, homes were scattered along the lake. Ruddock was the exception, for it was a town with a population of about one-thousand. Wagram, later called Napton, and Frenier were train depots along the tracks.

Ruddock had a huge sawmill which cut cypress trees from the Louisiana swamp. I have visited this site many times. The remains of the old sawmill now crumble and slowly sink into the deep, murky swamp.

Mrs. Burg told of a wonderful life- the kind most of us would like to live today. Everything was peaceful and quiet. There were no police because there was no need for them. No one even locked their doors. Everyone knew each other and helped each other as neighbors are supposed to do. Mrs. Burg told me that the residents were mostly of German descent and grew cabbage as their main crop. All of that farm land is now in the lake due to erosion. She also fondly spoke of times she would walk along the lakeshore for miles and how peaceful and beautiful it was.

The railroad came through the swamp in 1856 and made things better for the scattered home sites. Before the railroad, shipping farm goods or getting supplies was time consuming and difficult. Now, the train would stop when flagged down by residents. They would hand the engineer a grocery list. The engineer would drop off the list in New Orleans. Several days later, the train would again return to the swamp and stop to drop off items that had been picked up.

The photograph is of Mrs. Burg and her entire family,
taken prior to the storm. Mrs. Burg is one of the children
standing on the front porch steps.

Photo: Louisiana Treasures Museum

Mrs. Burg said, "All the groceries picked up and delivered never came to more than one hundred dollars a year. We raised our vegetables and would kill deer, rabbit, and other game found in the swamp for our meat. And, we always shared with our neighbors."

Once a month, on a Saturday night, a party would be held at one of the resident's homes. A different home hosted the party each month.

"We would play music, dance, and sing songs from late afternoon until morning," Mrs. Burg recalled with a little grin. "The Windecker boys were kind of bullies, and when they went to the dances, they would put alligator oil in their hair to hold it down. They smelled so bad that the girls didn't want anything to do with them. Oh, we had a wonderful time."

There was a community center at Ruddock where dances were held, but Mrs. Burg's family seldom went because it was a very long walk up the railroad track.

"We had no cars and no roads. We knew about LaPlace, but a five or ten mile walk through the swamp to get there was too much. Hardly ever would anyone attempt to go there unless it was to vote. We had no doctors, and all the babies were delivered by a midwife. Our mother treated us when we got sick. We had no electricity either, and our water came from a cistern."

Mrs. Burg told of the church and school with a sweet smile on her face. She said, "We had a Catholic church and a school- the Holy Cross Church and Holy Cross School. Those were small cypress buildings that stood on the west side of the railroad track. A priest would come from New Orleans once a month to hold mass. We had church every Sunday if we had a priest or not. School was held whenever we could get a sister from New Orleans. Whenever she came, the sister would catch the train that morning and return to New Orleans on the train that afternoon. It would cost her twenty-five cents to ride from New Orleans to Ruddock. We were very happy children and having the time of our lives."

Mrs. Burg sighed. "We loved where we lived in the swamp. I can remember it so well. Land was selling for twenty-five cents an acre. We owned forty acres back then."

The Ruddock train depot in 1903.

Photo: Louisiana Treasures Museum
(Courtesy of Tom Davidson)

Then, Mrs. Burg paused for a moment. With a serious tone, she explained, "One day, Daddy got the newspaper from the train and it told of a hurricane. Daddy said, 'You know, one day we are going to get a bad storm here.' We went to bed that night and had no way of knowing that our lives were about to change forever and, for some, this would be the end."

Mrs. Burg's father very likely read about the hurricane warning posted in the newspaper. However, back then, forecasts were not as reliable as they are today. Of course, even knowing of the storm's existence wasn't a guarantee, for residents would need a New Orleans newspaper from the train to know what was heading their way. And, even if residents were warned of the approaching storm, what could they have done? No one knew just how horrible the event would be.

With sadness in her voice, Mrs. Burg continued. "Wednesday, September 29, 1915, the day I will never forget. When we went to bed that night, it was cloudy. Later in the night, it started raining and the wind was starting to blow, but we didn't think much about it. Before daylight, the wind and rain were coming down very hard. My Daddy got up and lit the oil lamps. The wind was blowing so hard it just whistled through the large cypress house and would make the oil lamps flicker. You could see the waves in the lake hitting against the water breakers."

The wind and rain continued until about 9:00 am, and now the water was rising. Mrs. Burg described the event so clearly. "Water was all around the house and all the way up to the railroad tracks. The water had now risen about ten feet and the waves were hitting against our house. Daddy yelled to my mother, 'Get the kids ready, we are going to have to leave the house. I think it's going to wash away.' We had daddy, mother, and five kids in the house, and all of us kids were crying and scared to death. Daddy and my mother just kept saying everything will be alright. It's just bad weather."

Mrs. Burg recalled the small, cypress boat that belonged to her father. "All we had was one wooden boat, and Daddy knew that he couldn't take everyone on the trip. Mother said, 'You take some of the kids, and I will stay here with the others and you come back and get us.'

As we went outside to get into the boat, we had to hold onto things to keep from being blown away. The wind was now blowing over 100 miles per hour. Daddy put us kids in the boat and then just stopped for a second or two and looked back at mother. I know now that when he looked at her it meant 'I love you and I hope to be with you again.' I think he sensed it might be the end for him."

With misty eyes and much emotion, Mrs. Burg described what happened next. "The wind was blowing toward the railroad, and it blew us to the track in a minute. I thought the wind was going to blow us across the track, but Daddy jumped out and held the boat. He told us, 'Wait here. I have to go back and get Mother and the kids.'

It was raining so hard now that it was hurting us. We huddled together and put a table cloth over us so the rain wouldn't hurt as much, but then it blew away. Daddy was now trying to go into the wind, but he couldn't get anywhere. The wind just kept blowing him back.

We could see large waves hitting the house, and the house was starting to move! We knew if Daddy didn't make it soon that Mother and my sisters and brother would be killed. Daddy tried and tried, then finally got to the house. After everyone was in the boat, the wind blew them back to the tracks. We grabbed on to one another and walked, then crawled down the tracks to the school house.

My family went into the small school. It was dark and cold. The wind would whistle and howl through the cracks. Daddy and Mother kneeled down on the floor and started praying. The school was behind the railroad track, so Daddy thought the tracks would stop the water from coming. However, soon the water had risen twenty-five feet and was now coming over the tracks and large waves now started crashing up against the school.

My uncle and his family had now joined us. We were so scared. As the waves continued to hit the school building, it started to move. Daddy yelled, 'We have got to leave the school!' It was getting ready to blow away!

Again, Daddy loaded us into the small boat. He swam alongside us as we headed deeper and deeper into the dark swamp. Daddy thought that if we went far enough into the swamp, we might be safe."

Then, Mrs. Burg made a chilling statement. "We just knew we were going to die." After a brief recollection of her thoughts, she began again. "We had gone way out into the swamp when we heard the train whistle blowing. It was Train #99 bound from Hammond to Harahan. The engineer knew where everyone lived and was stopping at each home site, blowing the whistle so they would come and get on the train.

When the train got by the school and church, the engineer started blowing again. We were scared he would leave us. My family began to wave their arms and screamed, hoping the engineer would see or hear us. We paddled the boat with our hands. Just as the train started to pull away, someone saw us and yelled for the engineer to stop the train.

As we got to the tracks, we saw the school had blown down and was washing around in the water. We loaded into the train and then headed south, stopping at each house and picking up people." With sadness across her face, Mrs. Burg said, "I only owned one pair of shoes, and they got lost in the swamp. I was crying about it, too.

After a few miles, the train stopped. The engineer said that the tracks had washed away. So, he started to back up the train. We were back by the place where the school once stood and the tracks were gone there also. We were now stranded on the train with the tracks washed out in front and behind us. Waves were about 15 feet high and pounding against the train. Water had risen between 20-25 feet everywhere now."

Mrs. Burg's tone changed. I could sense graveness in her voice. "With water about two feet deep in the train, we could do nothing. Everyone kneeled down in the train, in the water, and prayed for hours. We knew a lot of our people were still outside somewhere in the storm. About fifty people had crowded into the train station at Ruddock and were on their knees praying when the building blew away. Everyone inside was thrown into the water.

Mr. Hazlegrove was the road master of the Louisiana Division of the Illinois Central Railroad. He had taken refuge in a section house occupied by Elardo and Mr. and Mrs. Louis Burg. They were on their knees praying when the front wall of the building blew down.

Everyone was forced back into the storm. Mr. Hazelgrove, to prevent a child from being blown from her mother's arms, insisted on carrying the child. He helped the mother and child into the train and then went back to the section house to rescue another child inside. As he started back toward the train with the child, he was singing a hymn to comfort the crying little one. Then, the wind just picked them up and blew them away. They were both found dead out in the swamp after the storm. The child was still clutched in his arms.

Peter Elardo, the last man to leave the section house, knew he was going to die. He said goodbye to everyone as he helped them get out of the falling house. As he helped the last person get out, a large wave hit the building. Mr. Elardo and the house were washed away in a few seconds. His body was found the next day way out in the swamp.

I remember George Schlosser and his twelve year old daughter, Lizzie Belle, were just swimming around when a dog house came floating by. They grabbed onto the dog house and floated on it for hours. Sometime during the night, the conditions became too much for them. They were both found dead a few days later.

We were told that Mrs. Schlosser hung onto an old boat and saved herself. Lydia, who was ten years old, held onto the roof of a chicken house until she was saved. Adam Schlosser and his brother George Schlosser were killed and buried under the section house when it collapsed on top of them.

Adam's wife saved herself by hanging on to the tin gutter of the second story of the house. Ethelney Woodsen and her two year old brother got into a boxcar for safety. The boxcar was carried about three-thousand feet into the swamp.

When they were found, Ethelney was holding on to the ceiling of the boxcar with one hand. The other arm held her drowned baby brother. Even though the boxcar was filled with water and only a few inches of air space to breathe, Ethenlney refused to let her brother go. September 29th was also Lydia Windecker's sixteenth birthday. Lydia and brothers, William and George, were killed by the storm.

Then there was an old black lady that everyone called Aunt Julie Brown. Aunt Julie was a big property owner and lived beside the tracks at Frenier. She always sat on her front porch and played the guitar. She sang songs that she made up, too. The words to one of the songs that she sang one day spoke of when she died, everything would die with her. Well, the day before the storm came, Aunt Julie Brown died.

All of her relatives and friends would board the train on September 29th from New Orleans. They were going to attend her wake. Aunt Julie was laid out in a cypress box at her house in Frenier when the storm hit. When folks realized how bad the storm was, they all tried to leave, but it was too late. Aunt Julie's body was found the next day out in the swamp. Only one man survived. Mr. Brown had climbed a large cypress tree. He watched seven of his friends being swallowed up by the waves as he clung to the tree. Mr. Brown said, 'Even with the wind blowing and the rain and noise all around, I could hear my friends screaming for help as they died.'

The storm continued through the night. Before daylight, everything got eerily quiet. The next morning, the weather was beautiful. The water went down and the lake was as smooth as glass. The sun came up big, red, and warm. It was one of the most beautiful days that I had ever seen.

People now started to come out of their hiding places to look around for their families. We could not believe our eyes. Out of all the towns, houses, and other buildings, there was only one structure left standing. The home of Theodore Grode had survived. It was sitting sideways, but it was still there all the same.

Trees were washed away, and the ones left standing had the bark stripped away. We only had the clothes on our backs, nothing else. Everything else we owned had washed into the swamp. Twelve miles of double railroad tracks had been destroyed. Train cars were carried almost a mile into the swamp. We were on the lakeshore and in the swamp with no food, clothing, water, or medical help.

John Ciro, an Italian man, and Milton Brown, a black man, survived the storm and walked for help through the swamp toward New Orleans. A relief party from New Orleans loaded onto the McMohen yacht, called the Lierline, with doctors, nurses, and medical supplies. They left New Orleans on a Thursday and reached us by Friday.

Another black man left Ruddock and spent two days walking, swimming, floating on logs, and fighting snakes through the swamp all the way to Ponchatoula and Hammond. He got in touch with a Dr. White from Hammond, and they sent a rescue party for us. While we were waiting for help to arrive, we had no food, so we ate the dead chickens that had drowned during the storm.

People just walked around in a daze. Some hoped to find their homes. Some were looking for their loved ones. There was a graveyard near the railroad tracks in Wagram/Napton. But, it was too far to carry the bodies of the dead. The men made rafts in the shallow waters of Lake Ponchartrain and floated the bodies to the graveyard for burial. Some of the people were not found for several days and were in such bad shape, they had to be buried in the swamp where they had been found.

We lost a lot of our family, friends, and neighbors. A total of 275 people were killed in Louisiana. The area around St. John Parish would have 13 white residents and 15 black residents perish during the storm."

Among the dead white residents were: R.L. Hazlegorve, 45; Peter Elardo, 34; George Schlosser,50; Viola Schlosser, 13; Lizzie Belle Schlosser, 12; Adam Schlosser, 45; Victor Burg, 23; Margaret Burg, 21; Joseph Burg, 62; Hilda Burg,1; Lena Windecker, 16th birthday; William and George Windecker.

Among the dead black residents were: Carrie Banks, 26; Gus Banks, 6; George Tester, 26; Blanche Tester, 24; Olevia Parks, 72; Hannah Burden, 70; Henry Clarence Woodsen, 6; Leontine Pierre, 32; Mary Clark, 40; Toddler Woodsen, 2; Infant Woodsen, 4 months; Rosa Feldson, 25; Rebecca Feldson, 6; Essel Young, 5; and one unidentified 30 year old.

Then a glimmer of hope came across Mrs. Burg's face. "I went back to New Orleans on the yacht. It was the most beautiful thing I had ever seen. Everything was so shiny and clean. I just looked and looked around. I was embarrassed because I was barefoot. I would cry whenever I thought about losing my only pair of shoes.

Track devastation after the storm.

Photo: Courtesy of Tom Davidson

When we got to New Orleans, we caught a streetcar to my aunt's house on Liberty Street. We lived there for two years. We did move back to Napton. My family lived in the only house that had survived the storm. We were the only family back there, and it was sad. We no longer had parties once a month. We didn't have our friends or relatives, so it was lonely. I relived September 29, 1915 so many times in my mind. Every time bad weather came, I would get very frightened.

This is the report from the *Times Picayune* New Orleans newspaper: (http://files.usgwarchives.net/la/plaquemines/history/hurc1915.txt)

```
30 September, 1915
New Orleans, Louisiana

The city emerges from worst hurricane experience - Barometer
lowest on record - wind velocity greatest ever reported.

The storm passed 20 miles west of New Orleans at 5:50 pm. The
Barometer read 28:11 at 5:50, 1/200 lower than ever recorded,
sustained wind velocity was 86 miles per hour in New Orleans.
Scarcely a house in New Orleans escaped without some damage.

OCTOBER 1, 1915

Death toll grows as news of storm comes into the city. Sections
south of New Orleans are hard hit. Devastation along Lower Coast
were a result of broken levees.

A radiogram was received from William McKeif, a staff
correspondent sent down the Mississippi River, read:
"Whole country between Poydras and Buras inundated. Levees gone,
property loss appalling. Life toll probably heavy. Conditions
estimated worse than ever before. Relief needed. No
communications."

There are known to be 23 dead in Venice, Ostrica, and other
lower river towns. At Frenier there are 23 and at LaBranch, 25.

This is a message received from a United Steamship near the
mouth of the river...
"A large portion of the lower Delta is a great sea.
Losses of crops are vast. Tidal wave was 12 feet high."
```

HISTORY OF THE STORM

The storm was first reported forming in the Caribbean Sea off the Leeward Islands about midway between Puerto Rico and the mainland of South America. Saturday the 25th, it was S.W. of Jamaica, moving toward the Yucatan Channel. On the 26th storm warnings were issued for Florida. On the evening of September 27th, it was moving north over the west end of Cuba. Tuesday morning, warnings went up for all points from Pensacola to Morgan City, Louisiana. At 3 pm, hurricane warnings said it would strike east of the mouth of the Mississippi River.

DR. E.L. McGhee of Hammond, Louisiana, Road Surgeon for the Illinois Central, who led a party of rescuers to Frenier, reached New Orleans at 2 o'clock Friday morning coming to the west end on the steamer, *Jessie*. They found the following dead: Roadmaster Hazelgrove; Adam Schlosser, and George Schlosser and wife.

Newspaper article from *The Daily States*, New Orleans on September 30, 1915.

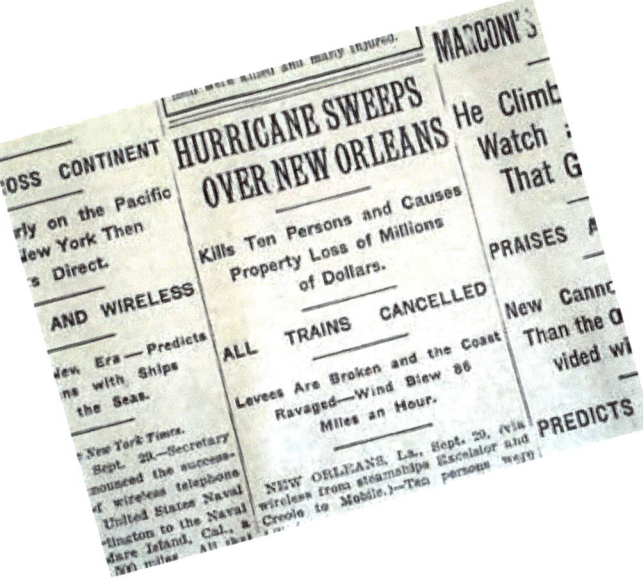

e New York
NEW YORK, THURSDAY, SEPTEMBER 30, 1915.—TWENTY-FOUR

LESS SPEECH RD 2500 MILES
Officers Telephone Message from Arlington to Mare Island, Cal.
ACROSS CONTINENT
Clearly on the Pacific Coast—New York Then Talks Direct.

Explosion Kills 242 Men In German Munitions Plant
STOCKHOLM, Sept. 29, (via London.)—The newspaper Dagens Nyreter, on the authority of a business man who has just returned from Germany, says that a great explosion occurred in an ammunition factory at Wittenberg, Prussia, on Aug. 23. Two hundred and forty-two workmen were killed and many injured.

HURRICANE SWEEPS OVER NEW ORLEANS
Kills Ten Persons and Causes Property Loss of Millions

FRENCH T 120,000 G ALLIES'
MARCONI'S STORY OF F
He Climbed a Tre Watch an Air B That German
PRAISES ALLIED

Newspaper articles from the hurricane of 1915 reported the extensive damage and loss of life.

Ruddock, La after
1915 hurricane

From Collection of
Tom Davidson
Hammond,La

Damage after the storm in Ruddock. Buildings and train cars were tossed like toys by the hurricane force winds. Ruddock would never recover.

Photo: Louisiana Treasures Museum
(Courtesy of Tom Davidson)

The railroad rebuilt the tracks using a workforce of 6,000 men. We moved from Napton a few years afterward to LaPlace."

Mrs. Burg ended her story with these words that I will never forget. "After we moved, the area, to this day, is still, quiet, and a forgotten place. But, it holds the memories of the storm that took so many lives and changed our world forever on that September day in 1915. I am happy here in LaPlace now, and I never want to go back to Napton again."

Mrs. Helen Schlosser Burg had told her story for one last time. She passed away thirty days after our interview from injuries she received after a fall and a broken hip. I am so thankful that I was able to interview her and record her story that will live forever in her own words. No one can imagine what these people went through to survive such a devastating storm.

Back in 1915, hurricanes were not given names. As a matter of a fact, hurricanes were not named until the 1940's. The first two named storms were George in 1947 and Bess in 1949. Hurricane Bess was named after the First Lady, Bess Truman. Before the 1940's, storms were named after a location or an event that took place during the time of the storm, such as Galvaston Hurricane or Labor Day Hurricane. During World War II, the practice of naming storms began to take shape amongst weather forecasters and Army and Navy meteorologists who plotted these storms over the Pacific Ocean.

A few last interesting facts about the hurricane of 1915. According to meteorologists, the storm of 1915 was a category 4 with winds as high as 145 mph. It was one of the deadliest storms until Betsy hit 50 years later. Then there was Katrina almost 90 years after the storm of 1915. If you were to lay the path of the 1915 storm on top of the path of Hurricane Katrina, you would see the exact same path!

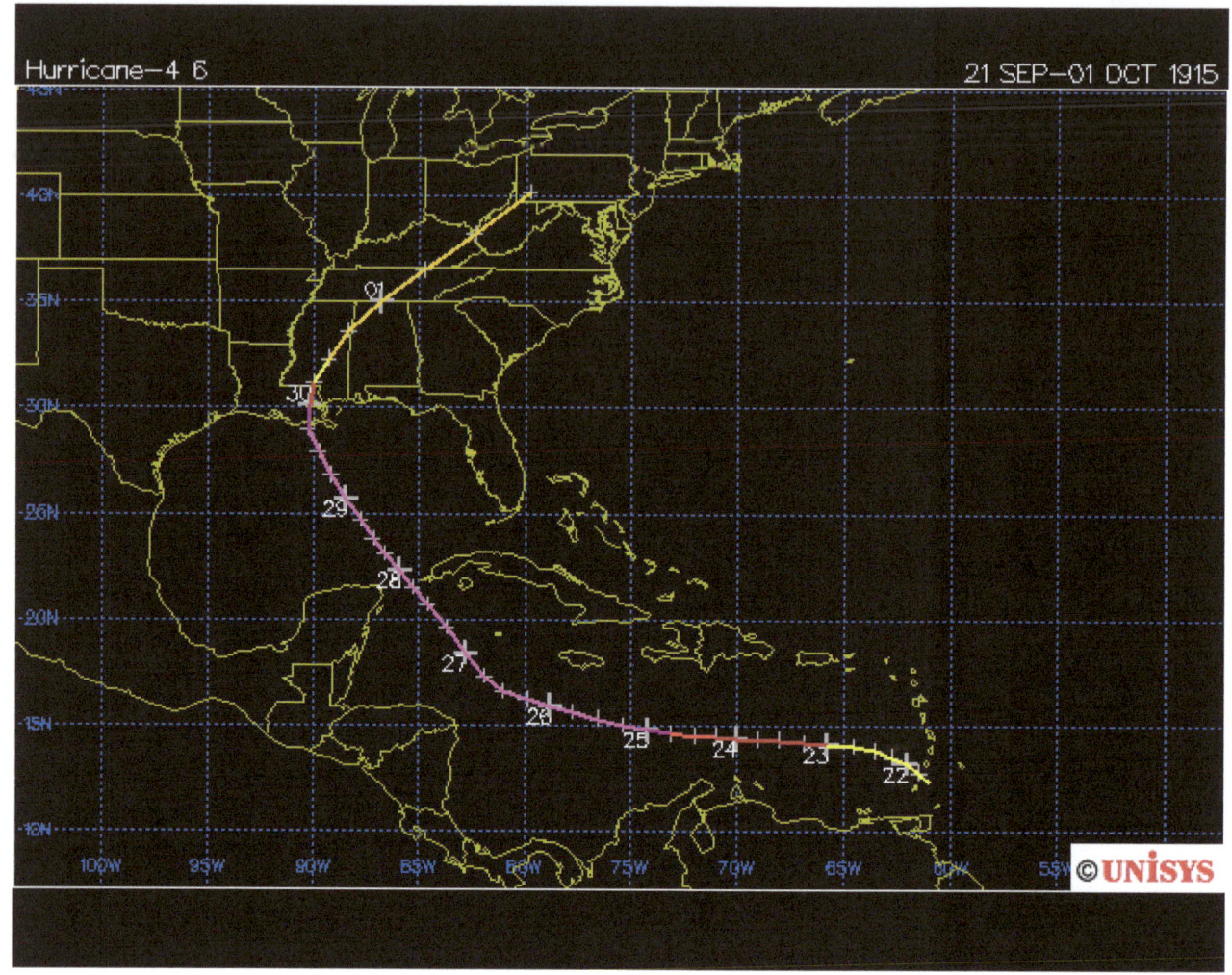

Track of 1915 hurricane

The Weather Channel visited the Louisiana Treasures Museum during the filming of a segment called "Voodoo Hurricane" which shed light on the hurricane of 1915 and the alleged curse of Aunt Julie Brown.

Photo of an area near Napton where treasures such as bottles, jars, dishes, bricks, silverware, and other remnants of the homes that were washed away by the storm can be found 100 years later.

Photos by: Wendy Woods

Treasure Hunting

For as long as I can remember, I have loved collecting pieces of the past. The area along the Manchac swamps have proven to be a vast treasure chest if one is willing to look.

It's hard to believe that remnants of these settlements from long ago still wash in and out with the tide along on Lake Ponchartrain's shores. Through the years, my searches have turned up some pretty amazing finds.

I built the Louisiana Treasures Museum to hold the treasures that I have collected on my dives and treks through the swamp. The museum has a vast collection of photographs, dishes, bottles, toys, and even parts of the homes that once stood in the swamps of St. John Parish. Many items recovered tell about the kind of lives the people of the past once lived. These artifacts help weave the story of the hurricane of 1915.

Mrs. Burg's story brought me to tears. She not only told me about the storm that struck their small town, but she also told me where everyone lived. She told me about her uncle's beer "shop" as she called it, with her little laugh.

Relying on a map that Mrs. Burg helped me draw, it's what I call my "Treasure Hunt Map." Hunting this area, I have found old bottles, butter churns, beer jugs, a lady's broach, an old iron, old bricks, and old tools, just to name a few of the items. So, the map really is a treasure map after all!

In honor of Mrs. Burg, I have all the items that I have collected on display in the Louisiana Treasures Museum. I am proud to say that the museum is rated 5 stars and every visitor to the museum tells me that it is the best they have ever seen.

I continue to hunt these towns and try to visualize what the people went through on that horrific night of September 29, 1915.

A collection of mason jars and miscellaneous bottles found near Napton (Wagram) and Ruddock on a treasure hunts.

Photo: The Louisiana Treasures Museum

A collection of jugs and crocks used by the residents of Napton (Wagram) and Ruddock.

Photo: Louisiana Treasures Museum

Top photo: Bottles, tools, and other items found near Napton (Wagram) and Ruddock.

Bottom photo: Bottles of all kinds line the wall at the Louisiana Treasures Museum.

FRENIER ~ 1917   Railroad Foreman's Home

The railroad foreman's house in Frenier in 1917 was being built. Recovery after the storm was slow. Most residents never returned to the area.

Photo: Louisiana Treasures Museum

Acknowledgements

Writing this book, telling Mrs. Helen Schlosser Burg's story, has been in my plans for years. This story was written in her honor. However, this book would not have been possible without the help, advice, and guidance of Wendy Duhe Woods. Wendy is a published author of Christian fiction and children's books, called the Indigeaux series.

Even in the middle of Wendy writing a new murder mystery book, "Dying to Know," she took out time to meet with me, proofread my material, and help me with the layout and photographs for the book. Thank you, Wendy, for encouraging me to finally write the book.

To my friend, Tommy Davidson, of Hammond: I would like to say, he is no doubt the most knowledgeable person I know with tons of information about the railroad. He has thousands of documents about the railroad, and is constantly contacted by persons all over the United States when they need information about the railroad.

I would like to thank him for sharing the photographs that were used in the book that show before and after the storm hit the small towns and changed their lives forever. Tommy has always had time to answer my questions or provide me material, and I thank him for that friendship.

For my wife of thirty-one years, Debbie Travis Norwood, I would like to say thank-you for your encouragement, input, ideas, and typing page after page of material that I had written.

Writing what I wanted to say in this book was easy, but typing it, I could not do. I could not even turn a computer on!

Without her love and support, this story would not be told and this venture could not have been made complete. Thank-you for working on this book with me, I Love You!

The Louisiana Treasures Museum is located on Highway 22 near Springfield. The museum is open every Saturday from 10:00 am to 4:00 pm and Sunday from 12:00 pm to 4:00 pm. Join our Facebook page for updates and details. For more information about the content of this story, photographs, and artifacts, please contact Wayne Norwood at (225) 294-8352.

www.ingramcontent.com/pod-product-compliance
Lightning Source LLC
Chambersburg PA
CBHW060836290526

45792CB00006BB/1950